HOW TO BECOME An "ULTIMATE NETWORKER"

George Dubec

"The Ultimate Networker"

© 2018 by George Dubec, Boca Raton, Florida 33487

ALL RIGHTS RESERVED. No part of this book may be reproduced, in any form or by any means, without permission in writing from the publisher.

About George Dubec

"The Ultimate Networker"

CONNECTING PEOPLE, PLACES & PROJECTS

Entrepreneur, Author, Keynote Speaker, Coach, Consultant, Trainer, Internet Marketer, Business Networking Expert

George Dubec is considered one of the top marketing and networking experts in the United States. He started his career in 1967 at Packard Electric, a division of General Motors, as an engineer and then became part of the management staff. There he gained eighteen years of experience in corporate managing and networking. He moved to South Florida in 1985 starting and operating the largest singles and dating network in the area, with over ten thousand people in his database. He gained experience, during that time, in social networking and matchmaking with the Find-A-Mate Singles Network. In the mid-90's, he was the vice president of marketing and sales for the Interaxx TV Network, producing a TV set-top box providing the Internet and enhanced broadcasting to customers. Over five years, he gained experience in corporate and B2B networking working with major corporations and retailers. He also helped in fund-raising activities for the company and networked with high net worth individuals and investors.

In the next phase of his career, he became the vice president of marketing and sales for WebStream Internet Solutions from 1997 to 2010. He helped make them one of the top web-design, online marketing, and hosting firms in the Southeast. He became an expert in networking with Fortune 500 companies, at major trade shows and social events, plus working with all types of businesses and nonprofits. He is a top connector in the high-tech world, which gives him access to the best resources available, all the latest cutting-edge technologies, and up-to-date programs, systems, and software.

After retiring, he became involved in entrepreneurial activities and developed several successful network marketing programs, earning over $25,000 per week, with thousands of affiliates in his networks. He learned to qualify prospects by networking and to recruit, train, and mentor hundreds of sponsored individuals. Other experiences included a national radio show, "The Internet Business Hour," which played in over thirty-five markets for over twelve years; developed a music and entertainment promotion company; modeled in movies and TV, and was the director of the Nightingale-Conant (www.nightingale.com) speakers' bureau for four years. He scheduled and promoted all the top public speakers in the country, such as Tony Robbins, Zig Ziglar, Brian Tracy, Dennis Waitley, Dr. Wayne Dyer, and more. This required networking with top companies and business leaders throughout the world.

Also, he is a recognized speaker and author presenting to groups, organizations, companies and at trade shows on a national basis.

Review his business experience and background at www.georgedubec.info. George is available for presenting, teaching, coaching, and consulting for business networking and online marketing. If you would like to contact him for services, call 561-777-3196, or send an
e-mail to george@georgedubec.com.

CONTENTS

INTRODUCTION 1

PERFORMANCE TRACKING INFOGRAPHIC 7

| STEP #1 | BUSINESS NETWORKER ASSESSMENT 10
(How do you presently rate)

| STEP #2 | WORKSHEET 24
(What do you need to do to become an "Ultimate Networker")

| STEP #3 | CHECKLIST 26
(How to prepare to network)

| STEP #4 | FOLLOW-UP 29
(How to follow-up and follow-through after meeting)

| STEP #5 | DATABASE 32
(Build a referral database "TEAM" and comprehensive E-mail list)

BY THE NUMBERS 35

SUMMARY 38

INTRODUCTION

Do you want to become an "Ultimate Networker" .... THE BEST OF THE BEST? I recently finished my book, "Ultimate Networking," which explains in detail how to do it (order on Amazon). Having said that, I realize in today's world people don't have the time or discipline to read and study a book. Thus, I have summarized and condensed the information into "5 EASY STEPS!"

Most of my family, friends, neighbors, customers, prospects, and associates don't understand how powerful networking is and how to network in an effective way. I estimate that most people operate at about a ten to thirty percent level of competency when networking and prospecting. I am using my years of experience to help others become better networkers with the information presented in this book. Follow the "5 EASY STEPS" and see how you will become more efficient and effective at networking to get what you want or need!

The majority of us are not educated or trained in networking, whether in school, at home or at work! Colleges and universities regularly give bachelor's degrees in marketing, business, and even entrepreneurship, but they offer very little in regards to the one subject that virtually every entrepreneur says is critically important .... networking!"

BUILD YOUR NETWORK BEFORE YOU NEED ONE

BUILD YOUR BUSINESS / BUILD YOUR NETWORK

BUSINESS IS A TEAM SPORT

It takes years to a lifetime to build a substantial network, but it will be the most powerful tool in your toolbox. A network is a compilation of all the people who are playing a part in your life. That would include teachers, repair people, club members, neighbors, customers, prospects, professional service providers, acquaintances, family, sports team members, mentors, investors, advisers, and anyone who has good contacts and resources.

Anything to accomplish of note requires the help and support of many other people. There is no such thing as a "self-made person." Achievements are made through a network of people working together toward a common goal. Building your network is one of the best investments you can make to succeed in life. As a great tool, to help you get started, I highly recommend you read, study and implement the strategies and concepts in, *"How to Win Friends and Influence People"* by Dale Carnegie. This is a time-honored classic and still has merit to help you relate to others!

That being said, you can buy all the books, attend seminars and webinars, plus get coaching, but it all boils down to the basics of action steps, timelines, and repetition! It helps to become persistent, consistent and relentless in your efforts. Don't be afraid or concerned if you start slow, feel uncomfortable or even fail. It is considered OK to be uncomfortable because you are moving out of your "comfort zone." Soon you will acquire new behaviors and find a new "comfort zone."

FOLLOW THE "5 EASY STEPS" AND IT WILL BECOME YOUR PATHWAY TO SUCCESS!

Networking

Business Networking

As a long time business networker, I thought I was very good. I initially rated myself as an eight on a scale of one to ten. After researching the content and writing the book, "Ultimate Networking," I completed the "Business Networker Assessment" and found that I only rated as a six. Even as good as I thought I was, I discovered a lot of things that I wasn't doing and other things that I could be doing better. It is a well-known fact that we should always be making an effort to improve ourselves and our skills. Once you decide to upgrade yourself, to become "The Ultimate Networker," you will get more leads, more qualified prospects, more customers, and more sales as well as have more success! You can also get a job, find funding for a business, find employees, and more. I recommend that everyone start building a referral network as early in life as possible. At any age, it's never too late to start. Becoming "The Ultimate Networker" means that you are THE BEST OF THE BEST!

Life Networking

You can get almost anything and everything you want through networking: a job, a spouse, ideas, a place to live, needed resources, and much more. Besides building a business referral network, you can establish a network of friends, associates, and resources who can provide and recommend services, ideas, and relationships. Whenever you have a specific need, create a detailed message of what you want and send to as many friends and associates as possible. Be sincere about it, and ask for their help; you will be amazed at how many will respond and the connections you will get. By using this method, you are increasing your search capacity many times over! If you use your network wisely, you will find out how much easier it will be to navigate through life.

YOU CAN GET ANYTHING YOU WANT BY NETWORKING

Six Main Reasons People are not Effective Networkers

1. Ineffective or poor follow-up and follow-through

2. Don't have a structured and organized referral network

3. Poor people, social and communication skills

4. Don't build strong relationships and help others get what they want and need

5. No training

6. Don't ask for help

Proximity Circle

List the top five to ten business people you communicate with the most during the month. You are the average of the group who you associate with!

YOUR NET WORTH = YOUR NETWORK

YOUR MOST POWERFUL TOOL, YOUR NETWORK

It's not only important to have a group of successful, quality people to interact with on a regular basis, but it behooves you to associate, as much as possible, with high caliber individuals. Networking is a circle that moves from a single point of reference (you) outwards to various levels.

Proximity Circle.....

- Close friends and associates (core group)
- Their close friends and associates
- Casual acquaintances and familiar faces
- Centers of influence
- Customers and clients
- New prospects
- Those you don't know yet but would like to

Make it your business to connect and communicate with high caliber, professional individuals at all levels. Go to events that have lots of successful people attending, which gives you the opportunity to make good connections and also to be seen at these events. You get credibility by associating with quality people and events! In other words, strive to be around the best people and places!

Performance Tracking/Timelines

To become an "Ultimate Networker," use the Performance Tracking system and be aware of the time element involved in the process.

Performance Tracking .....

>Assessment >>> Education >>> Training >>> Repetition >>>
>
>Habit >>> Reassessment >>> Implementation

Assessment..... (first step – one to two weeks)

- Starting point
- Review the areas from your Assessment that you rated low and would like to improve
    - List them on your "Ultimate Networking Worksheet" with action steps and timelines

Education..... (one to three months)

- Reading, studying, attending workshops, seminars, and webinars, plus watching videos on business networking
- Add strategies, ideas, methods and techniques that you want to incorporate into your "Ultimate Networking Worksheet"
- Read *"How to Win Friends and Influence People"* by Dale Carnegie

Training..... (one to six months – it takes at least twenty plus days to acquire a new habit or method of operating)

- Start following and practicing the actions steps listed on your "Ultimate Networking Worksheet"

Repetition..... (included in "Training" – must execute daily and/or weekly)

Habit..... (the after-effect of "Training" and "Repetition")

Reassessment ..... (after you have completed your "Training")

- You may backslide into old habits thus you must refresh yourself to get the desired results

Implentation..... (now you have integrated new methods and techniques into the way you operate)

Performance Tracking Infographic

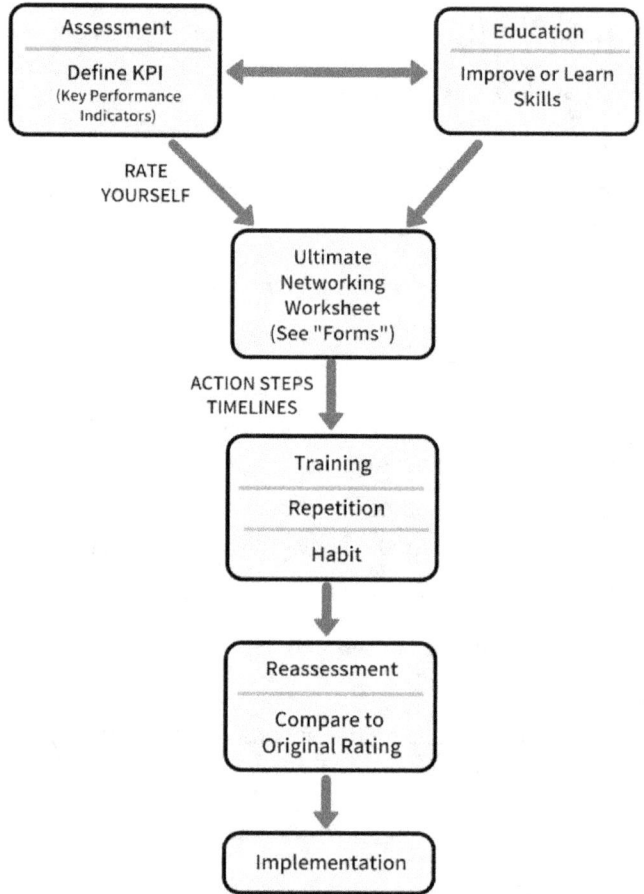

Timelines to Become an "Ultimate Networker"

STEP #1 | BUSINESS NETWORKER ASSESSMENT

- First step – within one week

STEP #2 | WORKSHEET

- One to six months, which includes completing the "Ultimate Networking Worksheet," education, training and repetitions
- After six months you should have developed new habits and methods of operating

STEP #3 | CHECKLIST

- Prepare in advance each time you attend an event
- Decide on your objective(s): meet new prospects, socialize, refer others, learning experience or discovery

STEP #4 | FOLLOW-UP FORM

- Complete during each event with new prospects and to-do list
- Follow-up within one to two days after event
- Follow-through within one to two weeks with further action steps that are necessary

STEP #5 | DATABASE

- Ongoing process that requires listing friends, neighbors, family, associates, clients and new prospects into a database allocated into specific categories (it will take about two years to build a good foundation for your lifelong database)

BECOME AN "ULTIMATE NETWORKER"

- It will take approximately six months to two years to change your habits and methods of operating to become an "Ultimate Networker" (depends on how much effort you put into the program)

STEP #1 BUSINESS NETWORKER ASSESSMENT

(How do you presently rate)

Rate yourself as a business networker on a scale of one to ten (ten being high). Then take the "Business Networker Assessment" (see below) to see how you actually rate.

Present Rating as a Business Networker _____

The most important part of becoming the "Ultimate Networker," or improving upon your present effectiveness, is to establish where you are now, how you rate on Key Performance Indicators (KPI) and then track your progress. Follow the "5 EASY STEPS" and work the program. Then retake the "Business Networker Assessment" after a period of time to see how much you have progressed. Take the test on a frequent basis to monitor your ongoing progress. Numbers don't lie, and the only way to find out if you are becoming a better networker is to measure your activities and effectiveness. You can choose which areas you want to improve and work on them (see "Worksheet") until you have formed better habits and integrated the principles—taught here—into your networking efforts.

HELP ME TO HELP YOU

The other aspect of networking is to help others find customers, resources, funding, education and more. When friends or associates contact you for help or resources, ask them to send you a detailed summary of what they need. Have them provide it to help you, help them!

BUSINESS NETWORKER ASSESSMENT

RATE YOURSELF AS A BUSINESS NETWORKER....

☐ Present rating as a Business Networker...scale of 1 to 10 (10 being high). Rate yourself on each point below ..... scale of 1 to 10 (10 being high). Circle your rating number on the scale as well as write in the appropriate box.

PREPARATION FOR NETWORKING

☐ 1. Establish your PERSONAL BRAND (see "FORMS")

```
0  1  2  3  4  5  6  7  8  9  10
```

☐ 2. Create a "Networker Profile" (see "FORMS")

```
0  1  2  3  4  5  6  7  8  9  10
```

☐ 3. Keep up to date on events in your area

```
0  1  2  3  4  5  6  7  8  9  10
```

☐ 4. Enjoy meeting new people and networking

```
0  1  2  3  4  5  6  7  8  9  10
```

☐ 5. Select events that will have prospects attending who are in your target market

|—|—|—|—|—|—|—|—|—|—|
0 1 2 3 4 5 6 7 8 9 10

☐ 6. Have a plan, establish your objectives and a time limit to spend at the event and with prospects

|—|—|—|—|—|—|—|—|—|—|
0 1 2 3 4 5 6 7 8 9 10

☐ 7. Invite friends, associates and customers to go to networking events with you

|—|—|—|—|—|—|—|—|—|—|
0 1 2 3 4 5 6 7 8 9 10

☐ 8. Find top networkers or salespeople in your category and ask them about their networking strategies

|—|—|—|—|—|—|—|—|—|—|
0 1 2 3 4 5 6 7 8 9 10

☐ 9. Have business cards, pen, notepad and/or a virtual business card (www.ultimatemobilemarketing.biz)

|—|—|—|—|—|—|—|—|—|—|
0 1 2 3 4 5 6 7 8 9 10

☐ 10. Rate the level of success of each of top 5 people you spend the most business time with each month on a scale of 1 thru 10 (10 being high). Then total the numbers of all 5 and divide by 5 to average the value of your business contacts

METHODS OF OPERATING

☐ 11. Create a name tag with your product or service displayed, along with your name

|—|—|—|—|—|—|—|—|—|—|
0 1 2 3 4 5 6 7 8 9 10

☐ 12. Meet with event promoter(s) and host(s) and ask for connections or referrals

|—|—|—|—|—|—|—|—|—|—|
0 1 2 3 4 5 6 7 8 9 10

☐ 13. Write legibly and complete all required information when filling in forms at networking events and trade shows

|—|—|—|—|—|—|—|—|—|—|
0 1 2 3 4 5 6 7 8 9 10

☐ 14. Create special promotions, discounts, offers and rewards for your products and services with expiration dates to create a sense of urgency

|—|—|—|—|—|—|—|—|—|—|
0 1 2 3 4 5 6 7 8 9 10

☐ 15. Spend your time meeting new prospects; not talking to friends and associates at events

|—|—|—|—|—|—|—|—|—|—|
0 1 2 3 4 5 6 7 8 9 10

☐ 16. Verify the credibility of new prospects and associates, so as not to waste time

0	1	2	3	4	5	6	7	8	9	10

☐ 17. When being introduced, ask about the other person's business and how you can help them instead of talking about your products and services

0	1	2	3	4	5	6	7	8	9	10

☐ 18. Qualify prospects by asking their level of interest in your products, services or projects on a scale of 1 to 10 (10 being high)

0	1	2	3	4	5	6	7	8	9	10

☐ 19. Ask open-ended questions when conversing with newprospects

0	1	2	3	4	5	6	7	8	9	10

☐ 20. Pay compliments to those you meet and network with

0	1	2	3	4	5	6	7	8	9	10

☐ 21. Take notes on your best prospects including their contact information as well as defining action steps, timelines and follow-up

|_|_|_|_|_|_|_|_|_|_|
0 1 2 3 4 5 6 7 8 9 10

☐ 22. Ask for referrals from those you meet, including prospects, friends and Associates

|_|_|_|_|_|_|_|_|_|_|
0 1 2 3 4 5 6 7 8 9 10

☐ 23. Collect business cards and contact information to add to your database

|_|_|_|_|_|_|_|_|_|_|
0 1 2 3 4 5 6 7 8 9 10

☐ 24. Introduce and refer new prospects to your friends, associates and Customers

|_|_|_|_|_|_|_|_|_|_|
0 1 2 3 4 5 6 7 8 9 10

☐ 25. Have an exit strategy ready to save you from long or boring conversations

|_|_|_|_|_|_|_|_|_|_|
0 1 2 3 4 5 6 7 8 9 10

FOLLOW-UP & FOLLOW THROUGH

☐ 26. Build a database of contacts and associates; update on a regular basis

0 1 2 3 4 5 6 7 8 9 10

☐ 27. Develop a network of top professionals who you can refer business to when you are networking

0 1 2 3 4 5 6 7 8 9 10

☐ 28. Establish a system to get referrals from customers, family, friends and associates (offer affiliate and reseller programs or other incentives)

0 1 2 3 4 5 6 7 8 9 10

☐ 29. Establish "Follow-up / Follow-Through" with a "Tickler File" system and Autoresponders

0 1 2 3 4 5 6 7 8 9 10

☐ 30. Follow-up with all qualified leads (within a couple of days)

0 1 2 3 4 5 6 7 8 9 10

☐ 31. Follow-through to close with all qualified leads after initial follow-up

|__|__|__|__|__|__|__|__|__|__|
0 1 2 3 4 5 6 7 8 9 10

☐ 32. Return all phone calls, answer all e-mails and text messages from new contacts expressing your level of interest in their products or services on a scale of 1 to 10 (10 being high). Then follow-up asking their level of interest in your products and services plus ask for a referral

|__|__|__|__|__|__|__|__|__|__|
0 1 2 3 4 5 6 7 8 9 10

☐ 33. Put in the time, effort, discipline, training and practice to improve your "Business Networker Assessment" score

|__|__|__|__|__|__|__|__|__|__|
0 1 2 3 4 5 6 7 8 9 10

RATING

_____ TOTAL (of SCORES above)

_____ AVERAGE (divide TOTAL by 33) = Business Assessment Rating

Rank yourself as follows ....

1 to 4 ....Weak (need help)
5 to 8.....Average (doing OK, but could do better)
9 or 10...Strong (getting good results)

BUSINESS NETWORKER SURVEY

1. If I needed to borrow $5,000 in a pinch, I have _____ people outside of my immediate family who would come through for me

    0 = 0 Points   1-2 = 1 Point   3+ = 2 Points

2. If I needed a non-monetary favor in a pinch, I can rely on _____ people that will drop what they are doing and help me

    0 = 0 Points   1-2 = 1 Point   3+ = 2 Points

3. I am a leader or hold a leadership position of _____ activities that are non-work related

    0 = 0 Points   1-2 = 1 Point   3+ = 2 Points

4. Within a week's notice, I could obtain _____ professional references. This time period helps determine how close the relationships are and how worthy they find you for an urgent response

    0 = 0 Points   1-2 = 1 Point   3+ = 2 Points

5. I regularly (at least once per quarter) stay in touch with _____ friends from high school, college, sports and/or hobbies, clubs and/or organizations

    0 = 0 Points   1-2 = 1 Point   3+ = 2 Points

6. I can confide in _____ people

    0 = 0 Points   1-2 = 1 Point   3+ = 2 Points

7. I can pick up the phone right now and call _____ former bosses and/or colleagues who would either employ me or connect me with someone else who would

    0 = 0 Points   1-2 = 1 Point   3+ = 2 Points

8. I have been asked by _____ people to be a reference

    0 = 0 Points   1-2 = 1 Point   3+ = 2 Points

9. I add at least ____ new person to my network a week

    0 = 0 Points   1-2 = 1 Point   3+ = 2 Points

10. How often do I grow my network?

    Never = 0 Points   Sometimes = 1 Point   Always = 2 Points

11. How often do I stay in touch with my network?

    Never = 0 Points   Sometimes = 1 Point   Always = 2 Points

12. Whether asked to or not, how often do I assist those in my network?

    Never = 0 Points   Sometimes = 1 Point   Always = 2 Points

13. When I meet someone, I think, "How can I add value to this person?"

    Never = 0 Points   Sometimes = 1 Point   Always = 2 Points

14. When I meet someone, I think of people I know that would be good contacts for them

    Never = 0 Points   Sometimes = 1 Point   Always = 2 Points

15. When I meet someone, I record and file their information within 24 hours

    Never = 0 Points   Sometimes = 1 Point   Always = 2 Points

16. I follow up with new contacts immediately.... connecting through LinkedIn, email, phone call, etc.

    Never = 0 Points   Sometimes = 1 Point   Always = 2 Points

17. When friends ask me for a good resource or service I can usually find one in my network.....sending an email, connecting with them on LinkedIn, making a phone call, etc.

    Never = 0 Points   Sometimes = 1 Point   Always = 2 Points

18. I make it easy for others to network with me by providing my business card, notifying them of contact changes, and informing them of updated details about me

    Never = 0 Points   Sometimes = 1 Point   Always = 2 Points

19. When I go to a networking or social event, I make sure I use the following checklist.....
    - Inquire about the attendance list
    - Research and prepare for the theme of the event
    - Go with a specific goal in mind
    - Have my elevator pitch down cold
    - Bring business cards
    - Bring a pen or something to write notes on the back of cards

    Never = 0 Points   Sometimes = 1 Point   Always = 2 Points

20. When I go to a networking event, I make sure I ask the host or promoter ahead of time who they think would be a good person for me to meet

    Never = 0 Points   Sometimes = 1 Point   Always = 2 Points

21. When I go to a networking event I will approach someone that I think would be a good person to know

    Never = 0 Points   Sometimes = 1 Point   Always = 2 Points

22. After I go to a networking event, I follow-up with new contacts within 24-48 hours

    Never = 0 Points   Sometimes = 1 Point   Always = 2 Points

23. I make it a point to connect with local celebrities, business leaders, politicians, business owners and heads of clubs and organizations

    Never = 0 Points   Sometimes = 1 Point   Always = 2 Points

24. I keep track of important details about my contacts regarding their family, hobbies, achievements, and special dates like their birthdays, kids' birthdays, holidays, anniversaries and other milestones

    Never = 0 Points   Sometimes = 1 Point   Always = 2 Points

25. The internet and social media is a tool I use to grow and stay in touch with my network

    Never = 0 Points   Sometimes = 1 Point   Always = 2 Points

26. I can tap into my network to provide a prospect, boss, client or potential employer with special information or an expert resource

    Never = 0 Points   Sometimes = 1 Point   Always = 2 Points

27. I have a network of people I can call on when I need help, advice, information or a resource

    Never = 0 Points   Sometimes = 1 Point   Always = 2 Points

28. I can easily find out when I was last in contact with someone by looking through my contact files

    Never = 0 Points   Sometimes = 1 Point   Always = 2 Points

29. I will have correct spelling, titles, and addresses for everyone in my network

    Never = 0 Points   Sometimes = 1 Point   Always = 2 Points

30. When I want to give a gift to someone in my network, I can count on my CRM to find an excellent idea on what the person might like

    Never = 0 Points   Sometimes = 1 Point   Always = 2 Points

31. My network is diverse as far as ethnicities, ages, religions, geography and industries

    Disagree = 0 Points   Somewhat Agree = 1 Point   Definitely Agree = 2 Points

32. I have strong centers of influence in my network who are successful and have leadership roles, are business owners and have a large database

    Disagree = 0 Points   Somewhat Agree = 1 Point   Definitely Agree = 2 Points

33. My network is very strong. I can connect with about anyone in the world

    Disagree = 0 Points   Somewhat Agree = 1 Point   Definitely Agree = 2 Points

34. How many people are in your close personal, professional, virtual referral networks combined

    <50 = 0 Points   50 - 100 = 1 Point   100 - 500 = 2 Points

35. How many people are in your contact database including social media

    <500 = 0 Points / 500 - 1000 = 1 Point / 1,000 – 2,500 = 2 Points
    2,500 – 5,000 = 3 points / 5,000+ = 4 points

36. How strong are your relationships with people in your close network (see item #30 above)

    Weak = 0 points   Medium = 1 point   Strong = 2 points

37. Are you actively building a "TEAM" of friends, family, neighbors, associates, customers and others who like you as well as your products and services. You also like them and their products and services thus want to mutually benefit each other. That means to refer business, brainstorm, mastermind, edify each other, share resources and ideas as well as communicate on a regular basis.

    No = 0 points   Starting the process = 2 points   Have a TEAM = 4 points

YOU'RE DONE!

Add up your points and review your present networking evaluation!

_____ Total Score

Evaluation:

0 – 25 .... Weak (need help)

26 – 50 .... Average (doing OK, but could do better)

50 – 70 .... Strong (getting good results)

71 – 78 .... Ultimate Networker

Note: This Survey has been adapted from NetworkWise (www.networkwise.com), "What's Your Networking IQ." Our adaptation of their qualified and researched Survey, was not analyzed or evaluated by any professional source or organization. Only use this as an indicator of present performance as it relates to business networking.

STEP #2 WORKSHEET

(What do you need to do to become an "Ultimate Networker")

How to Use the Worksheet.....

1. Where are you now?

Rate yourself on the "Business Networker Assessment" (STEP #1). This will let you know how you rate against the established standards of excellence to be an efficient and effective networker; THE BEST OF THE BEST............. "Ultimate Networker."

2. What is the "ultimate" way to be or operate (KPI – key performance indicators)?

Standards of excellence have been established on the "Business Networker Assessment" in each area and category of networking.

3. Do you want to become an "Ultimate Networker" to be better and more effective at networking?

Select the areas on the "Business Networker Assessment" which you rated low, and decide where you want to improve.

4. When do I start, and how do I do it?

Use the "Ultimate Networking Worksheet" and select the items you want to improve from the "Business Networker Assessment" and list them in order of priority. Then detail what action steps and timelines are appropriate to improve.

5. What is Performance Tracking?

After you have worked on your action steps, retake the "Business Networker Assessment" on a frequent basis and rate yourself to see how much progress you have made in specific areas.

ULTIMATE NETWORKING WORKSHEET

ULTIMATE NETWORKING WORKSHEET	RATING								
	TIMELINE								
	ACTIONS STEPS								
	STRATEGIES/TECHNIQUES								

STEP #3 CHECKLIST

(How to prepare to network)

A checklist is a listing of items you want to verify, check, or inspect so you don't forget anything. Using a checklist ensures that you take all the necessary and important steps before going into action. You should go over everything on your checklist and prepare any items you need to take with you, such as notebooks, pens, business cards, smartphone, camera, forms, flyers, worksheets, and any other items.

There is no perfect checklist, but use the "Ultimate Networking Checklist" as your guide to preparing for a great performance.

Also, decide on your objective(s) before you go to an event as this will dictate how you should prepare mentally, how to dress and what to take with you.....

- Find new prospects
- Meet new friends
- Get exposed to new experiences
- Have an educational experience to learn new things and get ideas
- Refer others
- Meet centers of influence and successful people
- Be seen at quality events by community leaders and credible individuals
- Have fun

After you review the "Ultimate Networking Checklist," it is time to go to work...

ULTIMATE NETWORKING CHECKLIST

- [ ] 1. Establish your Personal Brand (see "FORMS") as it relates to your main products, services, and projects

- [ ] 2. Complete a "Networker Profile" (see "FORMS")

- [ ] 3. Select a networking event, conference or trade show that fits your target market

- [ ] 4. Plan the strategies and techniques which you will be using to accomplish your networking goals and objectives

- [ ] 5. Invite a friend, customer or associate to attend with you (optional)

- [ ] 6. Business cards, smartphone, pen, notepad and your virtual business card (www.ultimatemobilemarketing.biz)

- [ ] 7. Dress appropriately to fit the event

- [ ] 8. Collect any and all the business cards you can (to input to your database) at networking events, expos and trade shows from sponsors, exhibitors, attendees as well as hosts and promoters

- [ ] 9. Meet the event host(s) or promoter(s) and ask them if they can connect you with anyone who might be interested in your products and services

- [ ] 10. Qualify prospects (those interested in your products and services). Ask what level of interest they have for your products, services or projects on a scale of 1 to 10 (10 being high)?

☐ 11. Have an opening line ready and follow with some casual conversation upon an introduction

☐ 12. Ask open-ended questions and listen twice as much as you speak!

☐ 13. Say your prospects name often and pay compliments

☐ 14. Have your "Elevator Pitch" and "USP (Unique Selling Proposition)" prepared

☐ 15. Take good notes and prepare to define action steps and timeline on a clipboard or in a notebook for follow-up

☐ 16. Ask about other's products and services, then inquire as to what they are looking for and if you can help them?

☐ 17. Ask for referrals

☐ 18. Have an exit strategy to leave unproductive discussions and meetings

☐ 19. Establish a follow-up system

☐ 20. Establish a follow-through system (includes "TICKLER" file autoresponders)

STEP #4 FOLLOW-UP

(How to follow-up and follow-through after meeting)

FORTUNE IS IN THE FOLLOW-UP / SUCCESS IS IN THE FOLLOW-THROUGH

WORDS ARE MEANINGLESS WITHOUT INTENT AND FOLLOW-THROUGH

BE CONSISTENT, PERSISTENT, AND RELENTLESS

Follow-Up

After meeting a new prospect or referral, don't leave without summarizing and detailing your conversation......

- Go over important points of interest, follow-up activities, and remarks.
- You might ask (as a trial close), "By the way, what is your level of interest in my product or service on a scale of one to ten (ten being high)?"
- Ask if you can "FRIEND" him or her on Facebook and connect on LinkedIn.
- Ask if you can add them to your e-mail database for future updates about your products, services, or events.
- Let him, or her know if you can connect them with a good referral for their product, service, or project, and discuss a plan to make the contact.
- Make notes on a notepad, in your smartphone, on the back of a business card, with the "Follow-up Form" (see below) on a clipboard or in a notebook.
- Establish a timeline/deadline for action steps. It is too easy to let things drag or procrastinate, which might cause the loss of a good prospect.

Find out the best way to communicate with the prospect in the future................

- Phone (main phone number—work, cell, or home)
- WhatsApp (phone app for phone, face time, or texting - www.whatsapp.com)
- Text messaging (mobile phone number)
- Social media—Facebook or LinkedIn messenger
- Skype (username)
- Personal meeting
- E-mail (e-mail address)

SPECIAL NOTE:

The benefit of using the "Follow-up Form" (see below) is that the prospect can see you arranging the actions steps and timeline for follow-up and this makes both parties more committed and accountable. Carry the "Follow-up Form" on a clipboard or in a notebook.

Ultimate Networking Follow-up

ULTIMATE NETWORKING FOLLOW-UP FORM				
NAME/COMPANY	CONTACT INFO	REASON FOR INTEREST	ACTION STEPS/TIMELINE	PRIORITY

STEP #5 DATABASE

(Build a referral database "TEAM" and comprehensive E-mail list)

If you don't already have a database for your contacts, start one as soon as possible. Add names and contact information daily as you meet people on a social basis or for business. You never know when you need to look someone up or find someone from your past. Use your contact list to start an opt-in e-mail database for promoting your products, services, projects, blogs, newsletters, and more.

A CLEAN, UP-TO-DATE DATABASE IS WORTH ITS WEIGHT IN GOLD

YOUR NETWORK CREATES YOUR NET WORTH

Build a Contact-List Database

- Add names and e-mail addresses to your CRM (customer relationship management) system and/or opt-in e-mail program daily, weekly, or monthly as you collect business cards and name lists.
- If you already have an e-mail list, make sure you clean it up by sending an opt-in/opt-out message.
- Don't buy e-mail lists or leads unless proven to be "clean" (a list of names screened as being opt-in). Also, always request a test sample before you purchase a list.
- Build a database whether you are in sales or not. Everyone needs contact information about others in today's world of constant communication.
- Find out the best way to communicate with those in your database e-mail, phone, Twitter, Facebook, LinkedIn, text, Skype, WhatsApp, or other and make a notation in your files.
- Collect business cards everywhere you go, and add them to your database.
    - (Entrepreneur Press, 2017)
    - Relationship Building Archives – Rich Habits Institute)

- (https://getcrm.com/blog/sales-statistics/)
- (https://blog.hubspot.com/sales/sales-statistics)

- You may want to get a business-card scanner if you accumulate large volumes of business cards......

  - Find business-card-scanner reviews at http://www.toptenreviews.com/computers/scanners/best-business-card-scanners/ or https://wiki.ezvid.com/best-business-card-scanners?id=bng.

  - Find business-card-scanning apps at https://appadvice.com/appguides/show/business-card-scanning-apps.

Relationship Building

[1] Develop a casual friend – 50+ hours

[1] Establish a friendship – 90+ hours

[1] Form a relationship – 200+ hours

FLOW (to sustain and maintain a relationship) – must communicate daily, weekly, bi-monthly or monthly.....

[1] Study conducted by Professor Jeffery Hall, University of Kansas (published in "Journal of Social and Personal Relationships")

Levels of Relationships

DO YOU WANT FRIENDS and FAMILY or a TEAM......?

Watch video - http://bit.ly/2BRYLhQ (video 2 min / 33 sec)

TEAM – those who you have come to an agreement to work together, support each other, refer business, exchange ideas, mentor and edify each other. Must not only like them, but like their products, services or business (keep in touch daily to weekly)

Top level – referral partners, clients, close friends and family members, centers of influence, mentors (keep in touch daily to weekly)

Intermediate level – prospects, good friends, associates (keep in touch weekly to bi-monthly)

[2] Approximately 15 to 50 people

Lower level – casual friends, family members, neighbors, associates, old customers (keep in touch bi-monthly, monthly or several months to yearly)

[2] Approximately 150+ people

[2] Dunbar's Number (research by British anthropologist, Dr. Robert Dunbar)

Developing Relationships

[3] (using sales statistics)

- 48% of people never follow-up with a prospect
- 25% of people make a second contact and stop
- 12% of people only make three contacts and stop
- 10% of people make more than three contacts
- 2% of relationships are made on the first contact
- 3% of relationships are made on the second contact
- 5% of relationships are made on the third contact
- 10% of relationships are made on the fourth contact
- 80% of relationships are made on the fifth to twelfth contact

[3] National Sales Executive Association

BY THE NUMBERS

Do not construe the numbers and statistics below as verified by scientific research, but rather use as indicators to make better decisions for your work efforts and time.

1) ..... [1] INDICATOR OF SUCCESS

- 15% based on skill and technical knowledge
- 85% based on the ability to interact with people and build relationships

2) ..... [2] READING AND MEMORIZATION

- One-third of high school graduates never read another book for the rest of their lives.
- 42 percent of college graduates never read another book after college.
- 80 percent of U.S. families did not buy or read a book last year.
- 70 percent of U.S. adults have not been in a bookstore in the last five years.
- 57 percent of new books are not read to completion.

3) ..... [3] SUCCESS WITH SYSTEMS AND COURSES

- Less than 10% of people actually succeed with any system, method or course.

4) ..... [4] BEST WAY TO ACQUIRE CUSTOMERS

- 85 percent said word-of-mouth referrals
- 2 percent said radio ads
- 1 percent said newspaper ads
- 9 percent said Google/Facebook ads
- 2 percent said direct mail

5) ..... [5] STATISTICS ON HOW MUCH WE REMEMBER

- WE REMEMBER 5% of what we get from a lecture.
- 10% of what we read
- 20% of what we see
- 30% of what we get from a demonstration
- 50% of what we see, hear and discuss
- 70% of what we say and write
- 80% of what we experience, practice and do
- 90% of what we teach others

6) ..... [6] SIX DEGREES OF SEPARATION

- 29% are able to make a connection

7) ..... [6] NETWORKING

- 91.4% of business owners said networking is part of their success
- 88 % of business owners never had a course on networking

8) ..... [7] HABITS OF THE WEALTHY

- 88% of the wealthy believe relationships are a key factor in their wealth. Only 17% of the poor agree.
- 67% of the rich believe in promoting yourself is important to success. Only 24% of the poor agree.
- 75% of the rich send thank-you cards or notes or email regularly. Only 13% of the poor have this Rich Habit.
- 72% of the wealthy volunteer five hours or more each month compared to only 12% for the poor.

[1] *How to Win Friends and Influence People* by Dale Carnegie

[2] http://mentalfloss.com/article/27590/who-reads-books

[3] Milana Leshinsky's Simplicity Circle (www.milana.com/blog/ there-is-no-guru)

[4] Alignable recently completed a survey of 7,500 small-business owners in North America

[5] Edgar Dale plus the Learning Pyramid from the NTL Institute, Bethel, Maine

[6] *Networking Like a Pro* by Misner & Hilliard (Entrepreneur Press, 2017)

[7] *Rich Habits* by Tom Corley - Relationship Building Archives - Rich Habits Institute)

RECOMMENDED

"56 Sales Statistics You Must Know in 2017 & Beyond" (https://getcrm.com/blog/sales-statistics/)

"75 Mind-Blowing Sales Statistics That Will Help You Sell Smarter in 2018" (https://blog.hubspot.com/sales/sales-statistics)

Summary

ULTIMATE NETWORKING is about getting everything you want and all you need through your referral network and by networking with others. Rate yourself as a networker based on how you presently think you are and then take the "Business Networker Assessment" to see how you compare to an "Ultimate Networker." After taking the assessment, review the areas where you are weak and then decide if you want to improve by using the "Ultimate Networking Worksheet." Over time, you will change your habits and methods of operation and become more effective and successful at networking. The next step is to build a personal brand; create a story to promote yourself and let others know who and what you are and gain prestige, credibility, and trust. Once you know what you want, share it with your friends, family, neighbors, customers, and associates and give them specific information as to what you are looking for and need. Help them to help you, which will increase your ability to get what you want. Before you go networking, review the "Ultimate Networking Checklist" so you prepare in advance. Once you have made contacts with qualified prospects, use the "Ultimate Networking Follow-up Form" to take necessary action steps and establish timelines for follow-up and follow-through.

Build your database and referral network on a consistent basis; never stop establishing new relationships, especially with influential and successful people, as well as maintaining and cultivating existing relationships. This book will be your guide in "5 EASY STEPS" to become an "Ultimate Networker!"

NETWORKING CAN HELP YOU GET MORE LEADS, MORE QUALIFIED PROSPECTS, MORE CUSTOMERS, BETTER JOBS, FUNDING FOR YOUR PROJECTS OR BUSINESS, FINDING A MATE, FIND NEW RELATIONSHIPS AND STRENGTHEN EXISTING RELATIONSHIPS

BUILD YOUR NETWORK BEFORE YOU NEED IT

BUILD YOUR BUSINESS / BUILD YOUR NETWORK

YOUR MOST POWERFUL TOOL, YOUR NETWORK

NETWORK WITH A PURPOSE

BUSINESS IS A TEAM SPORT

YOU CAN GET ALMOST ANYTHING AND EVEYTHING YOU WANT BY NETWORKING

HELP ME TO HELP YOU

PERSONAL BRANDING LETS EVERYONE KNOW WHO YOU ARE AND WHAT YOU ARE ALL ABOUT

BECOME YOUR PERSONAL BRAND

SELECT EVENTS THAT HAVE THE HIGHEST PROBABILITY OF FINDING THOSE YOU WANT TO TARGET

NETWORKING CAN GET YOU ALMOST ANYTHING YOU NEED OR WANT

* BE READY TO PROSPECT EVERYONE YOU MEET ANYWHERE, ANYPLACE, ANYTIME! FIND OUT FIRST WHAT THEY DO, HOW YOU CAN HELP THEM AND THEN INTRODUCE YOUR PRODUCTS AND SERVICES. HAVE YOUR "ELEVATOR PITCH" READY, BUSINESS CARDS OR VIRTUAL CARD AND QUALIFY THEIR LEVEL OF INTEREST IN YOUR PRODUCTS AND SERVICES FOR FOLLOW-UP AND FOLLOW-THROUGH*

THE KEY IS TO CONSIDER THAT YOUR TIME IS VALUABLE, SO MAKE THE EVENT AS PRODUCTIVE AS POSSIBLE WITH GOALS AND OBJECTIVES IN MIND; NETWORKING WITH PURPOSE

BOY SCOUT MOTTO ("BE PREPARED")

If YOU GET ONE QUALIFIED LEAD PER EVENT OR REFERRAL, YOU HAVE DONE A GOOD JOB

* YOU MUST GIVE TO GET AND LEARN TO ASK FOR HELP*

YOUR EXISTING DATABASE IS YOUR MOST POWERFUL REFERRAL SOURCE

YOUR NETWORK CREATES YOUR NET WORTH

REFERRALS ARE THE LIFEBLOOD OF MOST BUSINESSES

IT'S NOT WHAT YOU KNOW, BUT WHO YOU KNOW
IT'S NOT ONLY WHO YOU KNOW, BUT WHO KNOWS YOU
IT'S NOT ONLY WHO YOU KNOW, BUT WHO SHOULD YOU KNOW
WHERE AND HOW DO I GET TO KNOW WHO I NEED TO KNOW
WHO DON'T YOU KNOW AND WHO DO THEY KNOW THAT YOU SHOULD KNOW

IT TAKES YEARS TO BUILD CREDIBILITY AND TRUST, BUT THEY CAN BE LOST EASILY AND QUICKLY

DON'T JUDGE OTHERS BEFOREHAND UNTIL YOU HAVE PROPERLY VETTED THEM

DON'T READILY BELIEVE IN WHAT YOU SEE OR HEAR FROM OTHERS, BUT WHAT YOU KNOW IS TRUE

A CLEAN, UP-TO-DATE DATABASE IS WORTH ITS WEIGHT IN GOLD

THE FUTURE OF NETWORKING IS ONLINE AND MOBILE

FORTUNE IS IN THE FOLLOW-UP / SUCCESS IS ON THE FOLLOW-THROUGH

YOU MUST LEARN TO MAKE PERSONAL INTRODUCTIONS ANYWHERE, ANYPLACE AND ANYTIME

FACE TO FACE MEETING, WHEN NETWORKING, IS THE MOST POWERFUL TIME YOU HAVE AVAILABLE TO COMMUNICATE

CONVERSATION (what is said) IS NOT COMMUNICATION (to understand what is said)

TO BE AN EFFECTIVE NETWORKER, COMMUNICATION IS THE KEY

WEAR APPAREL APPROPRIATE TO THE EVENT

DRESS FOR SUCCESS / DRESS TO IMPRESS

PROPS CAN HELP YOU GET MORE ATTENTION; BE MEMORABLE AND STAND OUT FROM THE CROWD

NUMBERS DON'T LIE! IF YOU CAN'T MEASURE IT, YOU CAN'T MANAGE IT OR IMPROVE!

WHAT GETS MEASURED GETS IMPROVED

IT TAKES MORE THAN WILLPOWER TO MAKE CHANGE

WORDS ARE MEANINGLESS WITHOUT INTENT AND FOLLOW- THROUGH

BE CONSISTENT, PERSISTENT & RELENTLESS

YOU MUST TAKE CONTROL OF THE FOLLOW-UP ACTIVITIES AND ATTACH TIMELINES / DEADLINES

MANAGING THE PROSPECTING CYCLE CAN RESULT IN UP TO 50% HIGHER CONVERSION RATES

FOLLOW-UP AND FOLLOW THROUGH WITH TICKLER SYSTEMS AND AUTORESPONDERS

DEFINE YOUR SALES CYCLE FOR EACH PROSPECT, AND SET-UP YOUR FOLLOW THROUGH AND AUTORESPONDERS ACCORDINGLY

BUILD SOLID RELATIONSHIPS FOR LASTING SUCCESS

THE PROSPECT'S PERSPECTIVE IS YOUR REALITY

SUCCESSFUL PEOPLE BUILD NETWORKS; OTHERS LOOK FOR JOBS

ONE NEW RELATIONSHIP IS WORTH A POCKETFUL OF BUSINESS CARDS

A GREAT RELATIONSHIP IS ABOUT TWO THINGS; FIND THE SIMILARITIES AND RESPECT THE DIFFERENCES

RELATIONSHIPS MUST BE WIN-WIN

ACKNOWLEDGE THE GOOD DEEDS AND PERFORMANCES OF OTHERS

EDUCATION WITHOUT PURPOSE IS USELESS INFORMATION

ONCE YOUR NEW STRATEGIES, TECHNIQUES AND HABITS ARE DEFINED, YOU MUST TRAIN TO INTEGRATE INTO YOUR METHODS OF OPERATION

PRACTICING WITH REPETITION IS THE ONLY WAY TO GAIN NEW SUCCESS HABITS

PRACTICE WHAT YOU LEARN, LEARN MORE AND SHARE WITH OTHER

FAIL YOUR WAY TO SUCCESS

EDUCATION, INFORMATION AND IDEAS ARE USELESS WITHOUT PROPER IMPLEMENTATION

SOCIAL MEDIA IS THE NEW SUPERHIGHWAY FOR NETWORKING

*EVERYTHING ABOUT BUSINESS REVOLVES AROUND PEOPLE MAKING NEW CONTACTS, FINDING NEW PROSPECTS PLUS CONNECTING AND RECONNECTING *

A MAN ONLY LEARNS IN TWO WAYS; ONE BY READING, AND THE OTHER BY ASSOCIATING WITH SMARTER PEOPLE

SET A GOAL TO INCREASE THE AMOUNT OF TIME YOU SPEND ASSOCIATING WITH RICHER AND SMARTER PEOPLE

AS AN ULTIMATE NETWORKER YOU ARE THE BEST OF THE BEST

YOU CAN ORDER "THE ULTIMATE SERIES" BOOKS and "PROBE" games at Georgedubec.com or on Amazon

"ULTIMATE NETWORKING"
"ULTIMATE NETWORKING WORKBOOK"
"PERSONAL INTRODUCTION HANDBOOK (For Singles)"
"REALITY PROBE (Game Book)"
"SEXUALITY PROBE (Game Book)"
"REALITY PROBE – KID'S EDITION (Game Book)"

CONTACT INFO –
GeorgeDubec.com
Magic.vcardinfo.com
Ultimatenetworking.info

www.ingramcontent.com/pod-product-compliance
Lightning Source LLC
Chambersburg PA
CBHW070958240526
45469CB00016B/1617